SCIENCE Q&A

SPACE

— Edward Willett —

Weigl Publishers Inc.

Published by Weigl Publishers Inc.
350 5th Avenue, Suite 3304, PMB 6G
New York, NY 10118-0069

Website: www.weigl.com
Copyright ©2010 WEIGL PUBLISHERS INC.

All of the Internet URLs given in the book were valid at the time of publication. However, due to the dynamic nature of the Internet, some addresses may have changed, or sites may have ceased to exist since publication. While the author and publisher regret any inconvenience this may cause readers, no responsibility for any such changes can be accepted by either the author or the publisher.

Library of Congress Cataloging-in-Publication Data

Willett, Edward, 1959-
 Space / Edward Willett.
    p. cm. -- (Science Q/A)
 Includes index.
 ISBN 978-1-60596-072-2 (hard cover : alk. paper) -- ISBN 978-1-60596-073-9 (soft cover : alk. paper)
 1. Space sciences--Miscellanea--Juvenile literature. 2. Astronomy--Miscellanea--Juvenile literature. I. Title.
 QB500.22.W 55 2010
 520--dc22
                              2009008353

Printed in China
1 2 3 4 5 6 7 8 9 0 13 12 11 10 09

Project Coordinator
Heather C. Hudak

Design
Terry Paulhus

Photo credits
Weigl acknowledges Getty Images as its primary image supplier for this title.

Every reasonable effort has been made to trace ownership and to obtain permission to reprint copyright material. The publishers would be pleased to have any errors or omissions brought to their attention so that they may be corrected in subsequent printings.

CONTENTS

4   What is space?

6   What is the future
    of our universe?

8   What is the Sun?

10 What are sunspots
    and solar winds?

12 What are planets?

14 Is there life on
    other planets?

16 What is Mercury like?

18 What is Venus like?

20 What is Mars like?

22 What is Jupiter like?

24 What are Saturn and
    Uranus like?

26 What is Neptune like?

28 What is the Moon made of?

30 What are asteroids?

32 What are stars?

34 What are galaxies?

36 What is a black hole?

38 What are supernovas
    and quasars?

40 How does a rocket work?

42 What is it like to ride
    in a space shuttle?

44 Space Careers

45 Young scientists at work

46 Take a science survey

47 Fast Facts

48 Glossary/Index

What is space?

Outer space, often simply called space, is made up of relatively empty regions of the universe beyond Earth's **atmosphere**. Scientists think the universe started with a Big Bang—an enormous explosion—between 11 billion and 20 billion years ago. When we look up at the night sky, we mainly see tiny, twinkling lights that we call stars. They are just a small portion of the universe. It is difficult to believe just how far away and how big those tiny lights are.

Human journeys into space have revealed a great deal about space, although the farthest humans have traveled is to the Moon. Some unpiloted spacecrafts have traveled to the edge of our solar system. By learning more about the universe, we also learn more about ourselves and our own planet.

What is the future of our universe?

Some scientists predict that one of two things may happen to the universe in the future. It will continue to expand, or it will collapse.

■ Earth formed about 4.6 billion years ago.

The occurrence of either of these events depends on the total **mass** of the universe. We use the word mass to talk about how much matter there is in something. Every object in the universe has mass, and every object with mass has **gravity**. All objects with gravity attract one another. This means that, if there is enough mass, the universe has enough gravity to eventually stop itself from expanding and start contracting.

If there is not enough mass, the universe will expand forever. Scientists have added together the mass of all the galaxies and stars that can be seen by humans. They believe that there is not enough mass to make the universe collapse. However, scientists believe the universe contains invisible matter called "dark matter" that might give the universe enough mass to keep it from expanding. Nobody is sure what dark matter is or if it exists. It could be ordinary matter we cannot see, or something very strange we have never come across before.

What is the Sun?

Without heat from the Sun, Earth would be a frozen rock without plants, animals, or people.

At the center of our solar system lies the Sun. This solar system includes Earth and seven other planets. Just as the Moon orbits Earth, the Earth and all the other planets orbit the Sun.

The Sun is an enormous ball of extremely hot gases. It is more than 100 times the size of Earth. The Sun is very far from the Earth—93 million miles (149 million kilometers). This is a good thing, because its surface is extremely hot. The Sun is more than 100 times hotter than the hottest day in the hottest desert on Earth. Inside the Sun, the temperature is even hotter, an incredible 27 million degrees Fahrenheit (15 million degrees Celsius).

The Sun is also a star. It looks different from the other stars in the sky because it is so much closer to Earth than any other star. Some stars in the universe are as much as five times hotter than our Sun.

■ The Sun is so big that, even though it has been burning for about five billion years, it should keep burning for five billion more.

Total Eclipse

A solar eclipse occurs when the Moon passes between the Sun and Earth so that the Sun is wholly or partially obscured.

What are sunspots and solar winds?

Sunspots were discovered by Galileo, who risked going blind by looking at the Sun through his telescope. He saw dark blotches that slowly moved across the Sun's surface and changed from week to week.

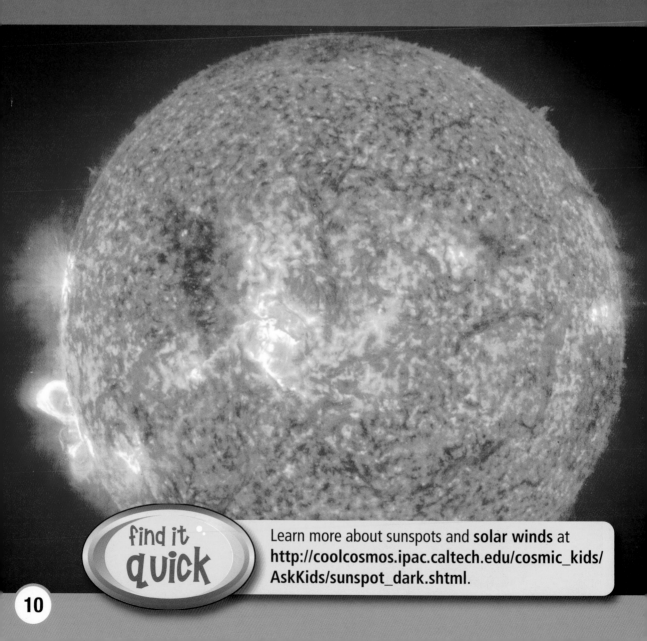

find it
quick

Learn more about sunspots and **solar winds** at
**http://coolcosmos.ipac.caltech.edu/cosmic_kids/
AskKids/sunspot_dark.shtml.**

For a long time, nobody knew what sunspots were. Although scientists do not know everything about sunspots, they do know these spots are not really black. Sunspots just appear black because they are much cooler than the rest of the Sun, which appears orange. Researchers also know that sunspots have very strong **magnetic fields**. Sunspot activity follows a regular 11-year cycle, going from a period with no or few sunspots to one with many sunspots. The sunspot cycle may affect Earth's climate. When sunspots peak, for instance, the southeastern United States seems to experience colder than normal temperatures. Sunspots are associated with solar flares, which are huge explosions on the Sun's surface. They occur in regions around the sunspots.

The Sun also sends out more than 1 million tons (907,200 tonnes) of gas particles per second. The solar wind takes about 10 days to pass by Earth. By the time it does, it is spread so thinly that there are only about 80 particles of it in

■ The northern and southern lights most often occur in the uppermost part of the Earth's atmosphere.

each cubic inch (5 particles in each cubic centimeter) of space. The solar wind is what causes the northern and southern lights. These are natural-colored light displays in the sky, usually observed at night, particularly at the North and South poles of the Earth.

Flare Flair

Solar flares sometimes cause problems on Earth. They can interfere with satellites and even cause power blackouts. A solar flare in March 1989 blacked out the entire Canadian province of Quebec and created vast northern lights that were seen as far south as the Caribbean.

What are planets?

Planets are huge spheres of rock or gas circling a star. Some of them are smaller than Earth, while others are much larger.

When humans first started looking at the stars, they noticed that, although most of the stars stayed in the same spot relative to one another, some kept changing their position. Ancient astronomers called such stars "wanderers." It was later realized that these objects are not stars. In fact, they were different. Scientists termed them "planets."

The planets in our solar system, starting from the closest to the Sun to the one farthest away, are Mercury, Venus, Earth, Mars, Jupiter, Saturn, Uranus, and Neptune. Most of the planets we know orbit our own Sun. Along with Earth, these planets form our solar system. Recently, scientists have discovered planets orbiting other stars. This probably means that many of the stars we see in the night sky are at the center of their own solar systems of planets and moons.

Our planet, Earth, rotates on its axis at approximately 1,000 miles per hour.

Out with Pluto!

Until recently, the total number of planets was nine. This included the farthest planet, Pluto. However, in August 2006, a panel of astronomers decided to vote Pluto out of the planet category, and the official number of planets is now eight.

Q

Is there life on other planets?

Three things are necessary for life: chemicals called organic compounds, water, and a source of energy. Earth is the only known planet to have all three.

find it
quick

Learn more about life on other planets at **www.windows.ucar.edu/ tour/link=/life/life_other_planets.html**.

However, some people believe that Mars may have had these three elements at one time. It is also possible that Jupiter's moon, Europa, has all three as well. The spacecraft *Galileo* took photographs of Europa's ice-covered surface that seemed to show places where water had welled out of cracks. This implies Europa may have a huge underground ocean. Hence, many scientists believe Europa is the most likely place in the solar system, other than Earth, where life might exist.

Mars does not have any life now, but it may have had once. Mars is now bone-dry, but it used to have plenty of water.

A **meteorite** from Mars was found in Antarctica. It contained traces of elements that could have come from ancient living things.

Humans may never be able to visit planets around other stars, but they continue to hope to find other intelligent life in the universe. For now, the only way we can search is by listening. Earth constantly sends radio and television signals into space. Other worlds may be doing the same. By scanning the sky with radio telescopes, scientists hope they might eventually hear a signal from some other solar system.

■ Many scientists have studied the possibility of life on Mars.

What is Mercury like?

Mercury is the planet closest to the Sun, so it is extremely hot during the day. However, at night it is three times colder than the coldest temperature ever recorded on Earth.

■ Mercury is the innermost and smallest planet in the solar system, orbiting the Sun once every 88 days.

Mercury looks like Earth's Moon, with craters, flowing lava, and dust-covered hills and plains. It is about one-third Earth's size, but has no atmosphere. Unlike Earth and most of the other planets, it has no moon of its own.

If you lived on Mercury, you would not see many sunrises and sunsets. Mercury's day, the time it takes to spin completely around its **axis** once, is about two Earth months long!

Here is your challenge!

Imagine you and your friends are planning for a trip to Mercury. Assume that all your basic needs of air, food, water, and warmth will be met by the design of the spaceship and the supplies that have already been stowed aboard. All you must do is decide what personal items to take to pass the time and keep yourselves entertained and happy. What would you take along?

What is Venus like?

Science fiction writers used to imagine that, beneath its clouds, Venus was covered with huge oceans and jungles. However, today scientists know that its atmosphere is mostly carbon dioxide. This gas traps heat from the Sun, making Venus's surface extremely hot.

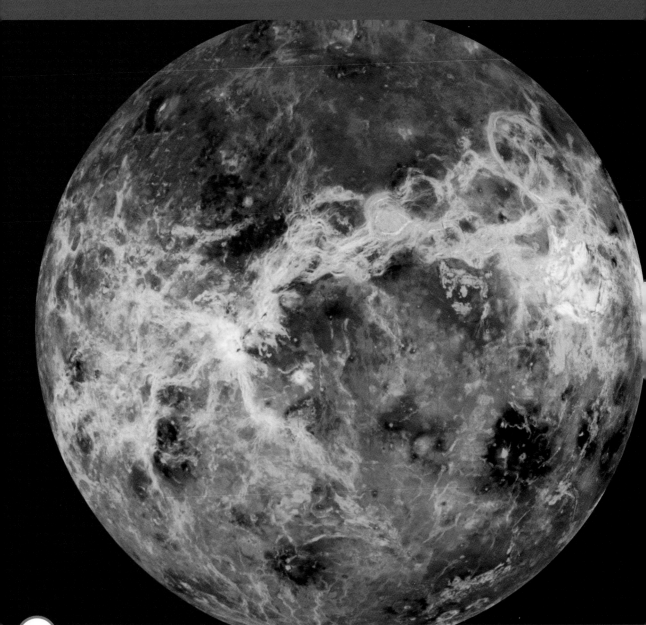

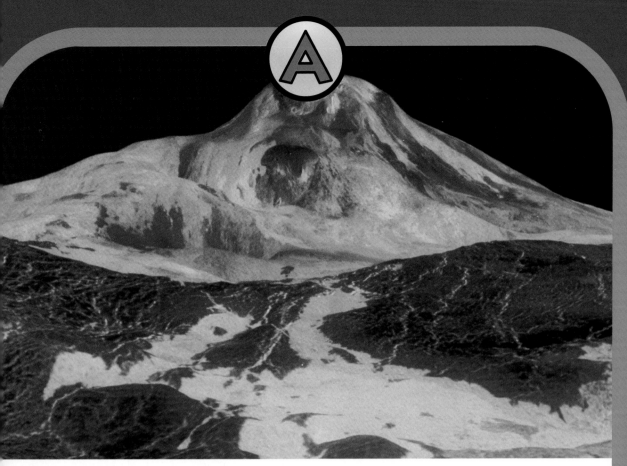

■ The surface of Venus is smooth in many places. However, it is likely to have many of the land formations found on Earth. These include canyons, volcanoes, lava flows, rift valleys, mountains, craters, and plains.

It is difficult to see the surface of Venus because the planet is constantly covered with clouds. These clouds reflect light very well, which is why Venus is the brightest object in the sky except for the Moon. Venus is almost the same size as Earth, but its day is even longer than Mercury's. A Venusian day is almost eight Earth months long.

That is Hot!

Venus is the first planet that a spacecraft from Earth touched down on. The Union of Soviet Socialist Republic's (U.S.S.R.) *Venera 3* probe landed on the planet in 1966. The U.S.S.R. went on to land several more probes on the planet. These probes quickly discovered that the surface temperature is hot enough to melt lead. They also found out that Venus's beautiful white clouds are actually made of sulfuric acid.

What is Mars like?

Astronomers in the 19th century thought they saw straight lines that were canals on the surface of Mars. For many years, people thought there was life on Mars. However, spacecrafts that have since visited Mars have shown that there is no life on the planet.

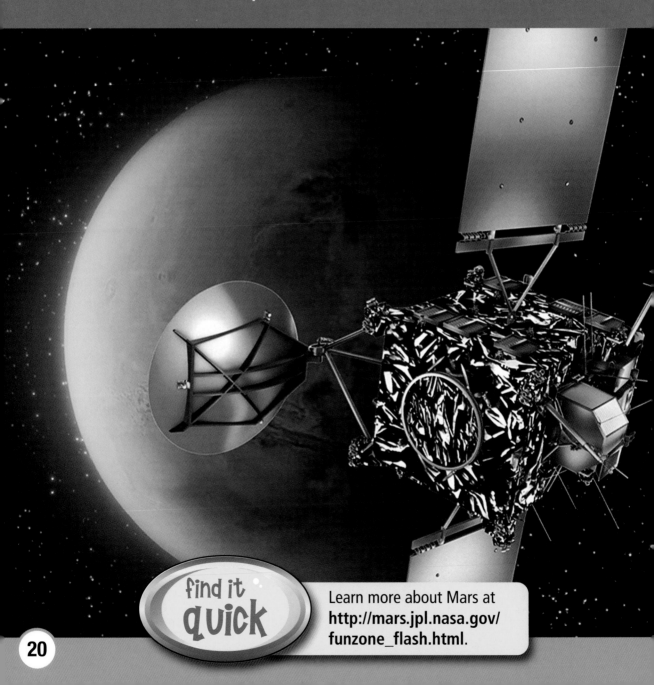

find it quick

Learn more about Mars at
**http://mars.jpl.nasa.gov/
funzone_flash.html**.

Although Mars, like Venus, has a carbon dioxide atmosphere, Mars's atmosphere is much thinner, with a pressure 150 times less than that of Earth. Although it can reach 80°F (27°C) at the equator, Mars is mostly very cold, with an average temperature of about -40°F (-4°C). Mars is only a little more than half as big as Earth, but its day is almost exactly the same length, lasting 24 hours and 37 minutes. It has two small, rocky moons called Phobos and Deimos.

Mars would be an interesting place to visit. You could go sightseeing at the solar system's largest volcano, Olympus Mons. This volcano is 16 miles (25 km) tall. It is almost three times as tall as Mount Everest, the highest mountain on Earth. You could also stop by one of the solar system's largest canyons, Valles Marineris, which is almost 4 miles (6 km) deep—more than three times as deep as

■ Olympus Mons would cover the entire state of Washington.

the Grand Canyon. However, you would have to be alert for giant, planet-wide dust storms that could ruin your whole vacation.

Mars Exploration		
Spacecraft	**Mission**	**Year**
Mars Odyssey	Orbiting Mars	2001
Mars Express	Exploring the surface	2003
Reconnaissance Orbiter	Orbiting Mars	2005

What is Jupiter like?

Jupiter is the largest planet in the solar system. It is more than 11 times bigger than Earth.

Learn more about Jupiter's moon Europa at **http://solarsystem.nasa.gov/planets/ profile.cfm?Object=Jup_Europa.**

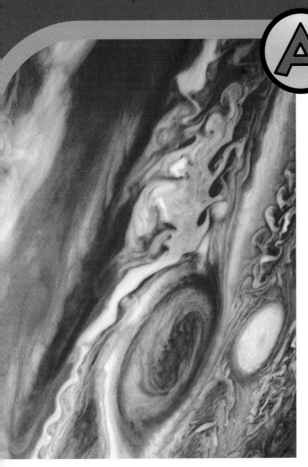

■ The Great Red Spot is an enormous hurricane that has lasted for at least 400 years.

■ Jupiter's four largest moons are known as the Galilean satellites.

Mainly made up of hydrogen and helium, Jupiter has no solid surface at all. No one is sure why, but Jupiter puts out more heat than it receives from the Sun. Most people think Saturn is the only planet with a ring around it, but Jupiter has a ring, too. However, Jupiter's ring is made of rocky particles so small that we cannot see the ring from Earth. Jupiter has 16 moons that we know of. Jupiter also boasts the biggest and longest-lasting storm in the solar system. The Great Red Spot, which has been in existence for centuries, is a storm similar to a hurricane. This hurricane is bigger than Earth.

Blast from the Past

In 1908, an object from space that was about the size of a house, hit the atmosphere above the Tunguska Forest in Siberia. It exploded, burning hundreds of square miles (square kilometers) of forest, and knocking down thousands of square miles (sq km) more.

What are Saturn and Uranus like?

Saturn is best known for its rings, which can be seen from Earth. They are made of particles ranging from tiny specks of dust to icy chunks many feet (meters) wide.

find it quick

Learn more about gaseous planets at
**http://news.softpedia.com/news/
A-Few-Facts-About-the-Gas-Giants**.

■ Saturn has more moons than any other planet in the universe.

Like Jupiter, Saturn is made of gas, and it gives off more heat than it receives. Saturn has at least 21 moons, which is more than any other planet in the solar system. It is slightly smaller than Jupiter, but still almost 10 times bigger than Earth.

■ Uranus is the only known planet that rotates on its side.

Like Saturn, Uranus, too, has rings, which are made of large, rocky chunks. The atmosphere on Uranus is much colder than that of Jupiter or Saturn. Uranus is also much smaller than Jupiter or Saturn, but it is still more than four times bigger than Earth.

Here is your challenge!

You will need a marble, a walnut, a golf ball, a raisin, an acorn, a basketball, a soccer ball, a softball, a grapefruit, a kidney bean, and sticky notes. Label the objects with sticky notes as follows: Mercury–marble, Venus–walnut, Earth–golf ball, Moon–raisin, Mars–acorn, Jupiter–basketball, Saturn–soccer ball, Uranus–softball, Neptune–grapefruit. Arrange the planets in order of increasing size. Now, arrange the planets in order of increasing distance from the Sun.

What is Neptune like?

Neptune's atmosphere is blue because it contains a great deal of a gas known as methane.

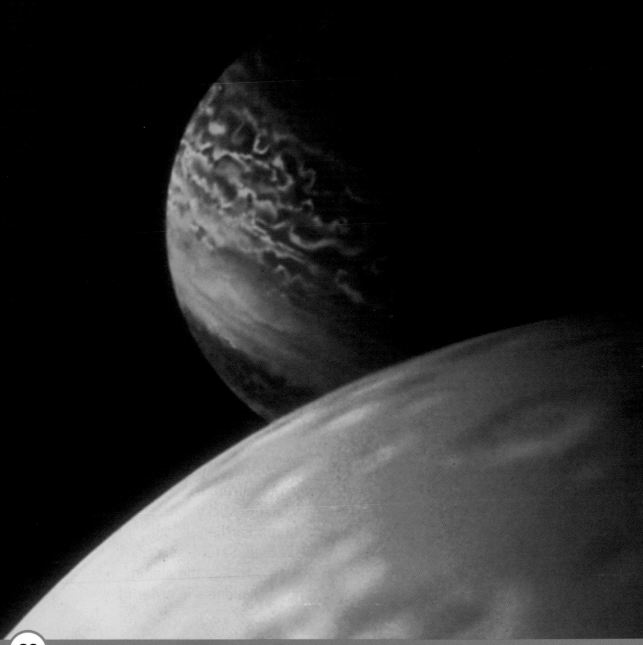

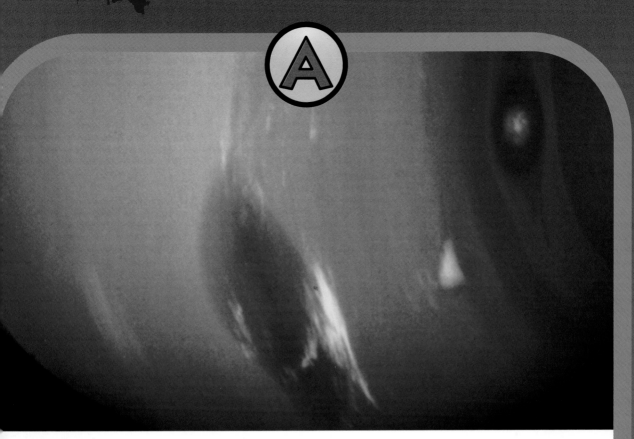

■ At first, the Great Dark Spot was thought to be a storm, but closer observation revealed it to be a dark, oval-shaped depression.

Like Jupiter, Neptune was thought to have a huge, permanent, hurricane-like storm. This storm, called the Great Dark Spot, is as big as Earth. Like the other big planets, Neptune has rings and at least eight moons. Even though it is farther away from the Sun than Uranus, Neptune is warmer. Like Jupiter and Saturn, it puts out more heat than it gets from the Sun. Neptune is slightly smaller than Uranus.

Beyond Saturn

The only closeups of Uranus and Neptune that exist were taken by the *Voyager II* spacecraft, which was never intended to go to those planets at all. *Voyager II* was supposed to go to Jupiter and Saturn, but after *Voyager I* showed that Saturn's moon, Titan, was covered with clouds and could not be photographed very well, NASA decided to send *Voyager II* on to Uranus and Neptune. *Voyager II* was given only a 30 percent chance of reaching either planet, but in 1986, it sent back pictures of Uranus, and in 1989, pictures of Neptune. It then traveled beyond our solar system.

What is the Moon made of?

When you look at the Moon, you can see its surface is not always uniform. It has dark spots and light spots. This pattern has made some people say the Moon is made of strange things, such as green cheese.

find it quick

Learn more about the Moon at
www.kids-and-space.com/sites/moon.htm.

■ There are many craters on the rugged terrain of the Moon.

The Moon is actually made of rocks very much like the rocks on Earth. The dark parts of the Moon are low, relatively level areas, covered with layers of a rock called **basalt**. They were formed when huge pools of lava slowly cooled. The lighter areas are higher, more rugged regions. They are made of many different types of light-colored rocks.

Like Earth, the Moon is covered with soil. Moon soil is made of broken-up rubble and powder that can be anywhere from 3 to 65 feet (1 to 20 meters) deep. On Earth, soil forms as wind and water wear rock away over thousands of years. On the Moon, where there is no air, soil has been created by meteorites crashing into and shattering the Moon's surface.

Meteorites range in size from tiny specks of dust to large asteroids that have blasted out craters in the Moon's surface. These craters are many miles (km) across.

Before people explored the Moon, scientists had three theories about its origin. One theory was that it used to be part of Earth. Another was that it formed near Earth. The third theory was that it formed somewhere in space and was captured by Earth's gravity. Recently, a new theory has been developed and has gained widespread acceptance. It states that the Moon was formed when a giant rock, called an asteroid, struck Earth. The impact spewed material from the outer surface of Earth. This material came together to form the Moon.

What are asteroids?

Asteroids are rocky or metallic objects that orbit the Sun. They are too small to be planets.

find it quick

Learn more about asteroids at
**http://space.about.com/
od/asteroids/a/asteroidinfo.htm.**

Asteroids are also known as minor planets. They range from the size of a pebble to 620 miles (1,000 km) in diameter. Most are found between the orbits of Mars and Jupiter, but they can turn up anywhere in the solar system. Asteroids were once thought to be the pieces of a shattered planet, but today, most scientists think they are raw materials that failed to form into a planet.

An asteroid on a collision course with Earth is called a meteor. Most meteors burn up in the atmosphere. Meteors that reach Earth's surface are called meteorites. Small meteorites have dented cars and smashed holes in the roofs of houses. Large meteorites can be much more dangerous. Earth's chances of a major asteroid impact in the next century are estimated to be about one in 10,000.

METEORITE DAMAGE	
DIAMETER	**DAMAGE**
0.4 miles (0.6 km)	On land, would cause earthquakes and fires over an area between 400 and 4,000 square miles (1,000 and 10,000 sq km). In the ocean, would create a huge wave that could flood surrounding coastlines up to 0.6 miles (1 km) inland.
1 mile (1.6 km)	Would cool off the entire planet by sending water vapor and dust into the atmosphere. Would block much of the Sun's energy and would damage the **ozone** layer.
1.9 miles (3 km)	Could completely destroy the ozone layer and cause a new ice age.
6 miles (9.6 km)	Would explode with a force 10,000 times greater than all the nuclear weapons in the world going off at once. Would cause earthquakes, turn the air burning hot, and make the Sun disappear for a year, wiping out millions of plant and animal species.

What are stars?

Just like the Sun, stars are balls of hot gas. Most are tens or hundreds of times larger than Earth.

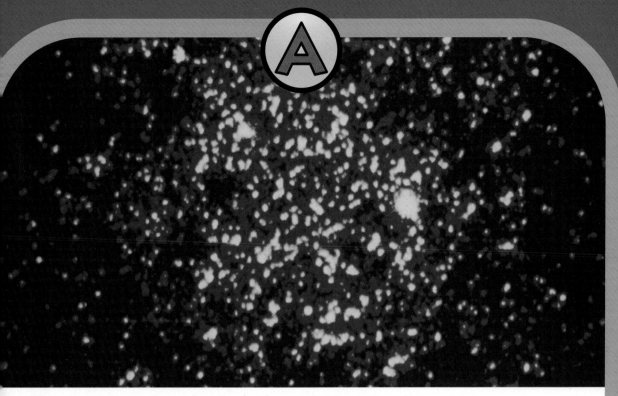

■ Star clusters are groups of stars that are bound by gravity.

Even though the night sky seems to be filled with millions of stars, only a few thousand can be seen with the human eye. Even the nearest stars are very far away.

The distance to the stars is measured in **light years**. One light year is the distance light travels in a year. Since the speed of light is 186,000 miles (300,000 km) per second, one light year is almost 6 trillion miles (10 trillion km). The star nearest to the Sun, Proxima Centauri, is a little more than 3.5 light years away. It is visible only in countries located south of the equator.

Light Years

When you look at a star, you are really seeing the way it looked many years ago, when the light you see started its journey to Earth. Looking into the night sky is like looking back in time, sometimes hundreds or even thousands of years.

What are galaxies?

Galaxies are collections of several million stars. Our galaxy, called the Milky Way, has billions of stars in it.

find it
quick

Learn more about galaxies at
http://spaceplace.nasa.gov/en/kids.

The Milky Way is only one among millions of galaxies in the universe. This means there are more than a trillion stars in the universe.

Galaxies come in a variety of shapes. The Milky Way is a spiral galaxy. This means it is shaped like water going down a drain. Spiral galaxies are the most common, but there are some that are oval-shaped, circular, or that have other unique shapes. Galaxies form groups called clusters. Our galaxy belongs to a cluster called the Local Group, which has about 30 galaxies in it. Many of these are very small. Some of them orbit around the Milky Way. The Milky Way is the second largest galaxy in the Local Group. The largest is M31, called the Andromeda Galaxy because it is found in the constellation Andromeda. It contains 300 billion stars. A constellation is a formation of stars perceived as a figure or design, especially one of 88 recognized groups.

■ Most galaxies are organized into clusters, which can form larger groups called superclusters.

Collision Course

Sometimes, galaxies run into each other, but the stars are so far apart that they rarely collide. However, the dust clouds in two galaxies can collide. This sends out shock waves that can damage stars in both galaxies.

What is a black hole?

When a star collapses, it sometimes turns into a **black hole**. A black hole has such strong gravity that nothing, not even light, can break free from it.

All objects in the universe from stars to planets to galaxies have gravity. Even people possess gravity. The more mass that an object has, the more gravity it will possess.

Individual people do not have much gravity because they do not have much mass. Earth has much greater gravity than human gravity.

Earth's gravity, in turn, is nothing compared to the gravity of the Sun, which holds the whole solar system in orbit. The Sun's gravity is also not strong enough to prevent light from escaping. If the Sun was much smaller, only 4 miles (6 km) across instead of 875,000 miles (1.4 million km), but its mass was the same, its gravity would be strong enough to stop light from escaping, and it would be a black hole. No one has ever seen a black hole, but scientists believe they have seen the effects of black holes in a number of places in the sky.

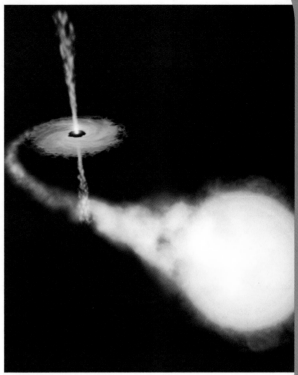

■ When a large star runs out of fuel, it can no longer support its heavy weight. The pressure from the star's massive layers of hydrogen press down, forcing the star to get smaller and smaller. Eventually, the star will become very very small.

Here is your challenge!

Go stargazing, and plot stars that appear in close clusters on a board. Connect the dots to make pictures of the different constellations. Then, compare it with existing constellations.

What are supernovas and quasars?

Supernovas are exploding stars. Quasars are an extremely powerful and distant active galactic nucleus.

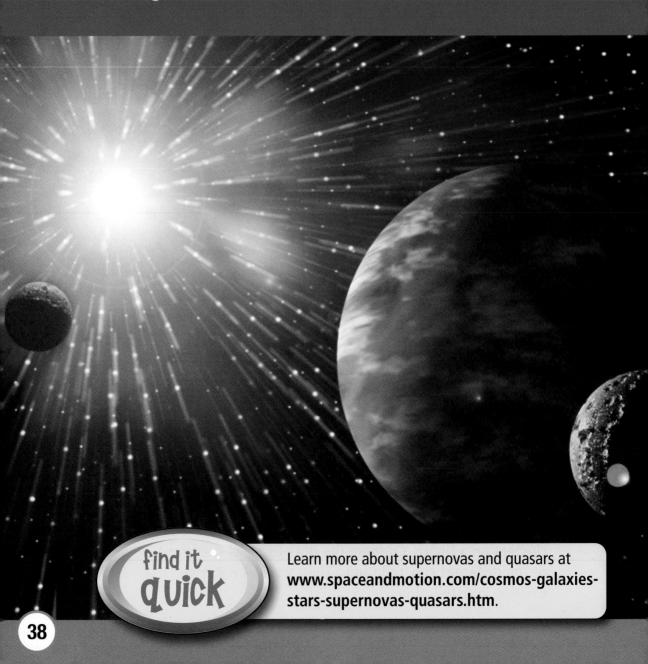

find it quick

Learn more about supernovas and quasars at **www.spaceandmotion.com/cosmos-galaxies-stars-supernovas-quasars.htm**.

Supernovas usually appear when very large stars burn out. They are 100 million times brighter than the Sun. When a supernova has finished exploding, it becomes a white dwarf, which is a small star that is not very bright. When a star uses all its gases, its core is a huge ball of iron, about half the size of Earth. This core collapses in seconds into a ball just 6 miles (10 km) in diameter. This releases a huge amount of energy, which blows the star apart.

Quasars are billions of light years away. Through a telescope, quasars look just like stars. They are very small, but they put out more light and more radio waves than entire galaxies. One theory about quasars is that each has an enormous black hole at its center, and that the light and energy are given off by matter falling into the black hole. Since many galaxies, including the Milky Way, probably have similar giant black holes at their centers, many scientists think quasars are the active centers of galaxies too far away to see.

■ The telescope was invented at the beginning of the 17th century. Before the use of the telescope, people thought that Earth was inside a glass sphere, or ball. They believed that the stars were simply holes in that ball. Light from the heavens could pass these holes.

Star Supernova

Some scientists believe that, if it were not for supernovas, there would be almost no elements in the universe heavier than hydrogen and helium. This means that Earth, and our own bodies, are mostly made of material that was hurled into space billions of years ago by exploding stars or supernovas.

How does a rocket work?

Rockets are the only method humans have right now of putting objects into space. The first trip to the Moon, and the first satellites, would have been impossible without rocket technology.

■ Fireworks are a form of rocket.

It takes a great deal of energy to overcome Earth's gravity. Rockets provide that energy. In a rocket, fuel and an **oxidizer** burn together. The oxidizer is important because it provides an important source of oxygen. On Earth, there is oxygen all around us, but there is no oxygen in space. Rockets are able to work in space because they carry their own oxygen with them. Burning the fuel produces hot gases, which are discharged through a nozzle. As Sir Isaac Newton, the great scientist, discovered,

"For every action there is an equal and opposite reaction." In a rocket, that means, when the hot gases rush out of the nozzle, an equal force pushes the rocket in the opposite direction. The rocket does not fly by "pushing" its exhaust against the ground or the air. It does not matter whether a rocket is on the ground, in the air, or in space. As long as exhaust is rushing out of the rocket in one direction, the rocket will move in the other direction.

Rocking rockets

Rockets were invented in China some time before the 13th century for fireworks and warfare. It was not until 1883 that a Russian schoolteacher, Konstantin Tsiolkovsky, realized that rockets would work in a vacuum and could be used for space travel.

What is it like to ride in a space shuttle?

On the rocket launching pad, you lie on your back with your feet up. In your mind, you run through everything you have learned through training to be an astronaut. You feel ready for any emergency.

find it quick

Visit the Kennedy Space Center online at **www.nasa.gov/centers/kennedy**.

When the countdown reaches six seconds before liftoff, the shuttle's three liquid rocket engines start. Although there is an ear-splitting roar outside, you can hear nothing inside the space shuttle. However, you can feel the shuttle shaking and swaying back and forth.

The count reaches zero, and a voice on your helmet radio says, "SRB Ignition – Liftoff!" Your shuttle's two solid rocket boosters ignite. The shuttle moves upward. The whole crew cabin rattles and shakes even more. You feel yourself being pushed back in your seat about as much as you do during takeoff on a jet airplane.

Two minutes after liftoff, the solid rocket boosters burn out and fall away, which makes the ride smoother. Three liquid-fueled rockets continue to burn. Since the shuttle has lost the boosters and is using up fuel, it is getting lighter and going faster.

By 7.5 minutes into the flight, the shuttle weighs only one-tenth what it did at launch, and you feel like you weigh three times as much as you do on Earth, making it hard to even breathe. At this point, the engines are throttled down so

Astronauts must become familiar with the shuttle's many controls.

the acceleration does not increase, and the astronauts do not feel any heavier.

Finally, the main engines cut off. The thrust stops, and you suddenly find yourself weightless. You are in space.

Space Careers

Astronaut

To be an astronaut, it is important that you are physically fit. You also must have a university education and three years of related experience. If you want to be an astronaut pilot, you have to learn to fly jets first. Pilots must have at least 1,000 hours of experience flying jets, and they must have perfect vision. Finally, you have to apply for the astronaut program. On average, more than 4,000 people apply for about 20 openings that become available every two years.

Astronomer

An astronomer is a scientist who studies outer space and the objects found there. To be an astronomer, you need to be good at mathematics and have the ability to think logically. You also have to be able to use a computer. Astronomers are very patient and determined. They often spend years trying to figure out the answer to a particular problem. To explain your discoveries to other people, you need to be able to write and speak in a clear, interesting way. You can learn many of these skills through proper education and training.

find it
quick

Learn more about space careers at **mgs-mager.gsfc.nasa.gov/ Kids/careers.html**.

Young scientists at work

FACT

The Moon appears to change shape at different times of the month. This change happens because of the changes in the Moon's position in its orbit around Earth, and because of its relationship to the Sun's light.

TEST

While sitting in a darkened room, have a friend or family member hold a ball at different positions around a lamp. From where you are sitting, what are the differences in the illumination of the ball at each point around the lamp? Does the shape of the lighted area change depending on where the ball is held?

FACT

Long ago, people told stories about the "pictures" they saw in the night sky. Many star groups were named after the people, animals, and objects that our ancestors imagined when they looked at the stars.

TEST

Use your imagination and some art supplies to create pictures and stories of the star patterns you see in the night sky.

Take a science survey

Imagine you have the opportunity to plan and build a space station that will orbit Earth, where ordinary people can live and work. There are many things to consider in your plans. For example, you would have to decide what type of food to take, how you would remove waste, and how to have a constant supply of clean drinking water. Do some brainstorming by yourself, or with your friends or family. Try to think of the things you would need to have on your space station. Then, answer the survey questions below.

WHAT ARE YOUR ANSWERS?

1. List as many things as you can think of that you would need to survive in space. Remember the things that we take for granted here on Earth that are essential to our survival in space.

2. What types of food would you need to produce on your space station? Would there be anything that you would have to transport from Earth?

3. What would you do with all of the garbage and waste that would be produced on your space station? Try to think of some ways to reuse and recycle items that would normally be thrown out as trash on Earth.

4. What would you do if there were an emergency on your space station? How would you get everybody safely back to Earth?

5. Who would you need to work with on your space station? Think of some of the people who would help you keep things running smoothly.

6. Where would the power for your space station come from?

Fast Facts

A space shuttle travels at approximately 5 miles (8 km) per second.

Food tastes different in space. Some astronauts find that, in space, they hate to eat the foods they normally like on Earth.

If your school were located on the Moon, it would take you 4 months, 29 days, 6 hours, and 10 minutes to get there if your school bus was traveling at a constant speed of 65 miles per hour (100 kph).

When a comet approaches the Sun, its tail is following it. When it moves away from the Sun, its tail is in front of it.

The Milky Way galaxy is so big that light, traveling at 186,000 miles (300,000 km) per second, still takes 75,000 years to travel from one side of the galaxy to the other.

You can tell how hot a star is by its color. Blue stars are hotter than yellow stars, which are hotter than red stars.

Mercury has the widest range in temperatures of any planet in the solar system. On the sunlit side, it can reach 864°F (462°C), while at the same time, the dark side is at -298°F (-183°C).

Overall, Venus is the hottest planet in the solar system. Its surface temperature everywhere is 867°F (464°C), which is hot enough to melt lead.

The Sun is so much bigger than the planets that it contains 99 percent of the solar system's total mass.

The Sun loses 8 million tons (7,257,478 tonnes) of gas every 2 seconds.

Glossary

atmosphere: the layer of air surrounding Earth

axis: the imaginary line that runs through the center of Earth

basalt: a type of rock that is very dark in color

black hole: a region in space produced by the collapse of a star

gravity: a force of attraction that draws two objects together

light years: the distance traveled by light in one year

magnetic fields: the force around a magnet

mass: the amount of matter in an object

meteorite: a meteor that reaches Earth before burning up in the atmosphere

oxidizer: a chemical that provides a source of oxygen

ozone: the gas that forms a layer of the atmosphere. Ozone absorbs ultraviolet radiation from the Sun and protects Earth

solar wind: the flow of gases given off by the Sun into space

Index

asteroid 29, 30, 31
astronauts 41, 42, 43, 44, 45
astronomers 13, 20, 44

black hole 36, 37, 39

galaxy 34, 35, 47
gravity 7, 29, 33, 36, 37, 41
Great Red Spot 23

meteorite 15, 29, 31
Milky Way 34, 35, 39, 47

northern lights 11

rocket 40, 41, 42, 43

satellites 11, 23, 40
space shuttle 42, 43, 47
sunspots 10, 11